water & spirit

# DEVOTIONS FOR LENT
## 2023

AUGSBURG FORTRESS

Minneapolis

WATER AND SPIRIT
Devotions for Lent 2023

pISBN 978-1-5064-8803-5
eISBN 978-1-5064-9124-0

Writers: Paul E. Hoffman (February 22–March 4), Michael Coffey (March 5–11), Jennifer L. Phelps (March 12–16), Annabelle Peake Markey (March 17–23), Felix Javier Malpica (March 24–31), Meghan Johnston Aelabouni (April 1–8)

Editor: Laurie J. Hanson
Cover design: Alisha Lofgren
Cover and interior images: All images © Getty Images. Used by permission.
Interior design and typesetting: Eileen Engebretson

The paper used in this publication meets the minimum requirements of American National Standard for Information Sciences—Permanence of Paper for Printed Library Materials, ANSI Z329.48-1984.

Manufactured in the USA.

23   22                                              1   2   3   4   5

# Welcome

*Water and Spirit* provides daily devotions for each day from Ash Wednesday to the Resurrection of Our Lord/Vigil of Easter (traditionally known as Holy Saturday). Devotions begin with an evocative image and a brief passage from the Gospel of John. The writers then bring their unique voices and pastoral wisdom to the texts with quotations to ponder, reflections, and prayers.

For year A the Revised Common Lectionary assigns texts from John's gospel to the second through fifth Sundays in Lent, as well Maundy Thursday, Good Friday, and the Vigil of Easter. These texts are included in this devotional. Several of them are unique to John: Jesus urges Nicodemus to be born again "of water and spirit," offers "living water" to a Samaritan woman at the well, raises Lazarus from the dead, washes the disciples' feet, and surprises Mary Magdalene at the empty tomb. As you read the daily devotions, pause to think about how John describes water and the Spirit, and how water and the Spirit are at work in your life.

May Christ's living water and the Spirit's power accompany you on this journey through Lent to the Easter feast.

## John 1:1-4

In the beginning was the Word, and the Word was with God, and the Word was God. He was in the beginning with God. All things came into being through him, and without him not one thing came into being. What has come into being in him was life, and the life was the light of all people.

## To ponder

In my end is my beginning.—T. S. Eliot, *Four Quartets*

## Nothing muffled about these drums

In the beginning was the Word. When humanity was formed from the dust of the earth, Christ was there. When we return to our parent dust, Christ will be there. Most pertinent to this day is the reminder that Christ is with us each step of our journey, even though, as Longfellow says, "our hearts, . . . like muffled drums, are beating funeral marches to the grave."

Lent is a journey through the cross of Jesus to the grave. There is nothing muffled about that message. We cannot escape what Ash Wednesday proclaims: we are dust, and to dust we shall return. But through the power of the One who was present at creation, the grave to which we are headed is just not any grave. It is an *empty* grave, the grave left forever defeated by the resurrection of Jesus, through whom all things were not only made, but through whom all things have been *remade*.

By the gift of water and the Spirit in our baptisms into Christ's death and resurrection, our end is our beginning. Each day of the Lenten season will be a day on that seemingly contradictory road. In the cross is victory; in death, resurrection; in our end, a new beginning through Christ, the life and light of all people.

## Prayer

Lord Jesus, our end and our beginning, thank you for the gift of baptism. United with you in a death like yours, we shall certainly be united with you in a resurrection like yours. Empower us to walk each day with the wisdom of our death to sin and our rising to new life in you. Amen.

## February 23

### John 1:14, 16-17

And the Word because flesh and lived among us, and we have seen his glory, the glory as of a father's only son, full of grace and truth. . . . From his fullness we have all received, grace upon grace. The law indeed was given through Moses; grace and truth came through Jesus Christ.

### To ponder

Amazing grace!—how sweet the sound—
that saved a wretch like me!
—"Amazing grace, how sweet the sound," ELW 779

## A wretch like me

Were someone to call me a wretch, I would take offense. Yet I sing "Amazing grace!" with gusto, seldom stopping to consider how its first twelve words contain the paradox of a life of faith. In the law we wretches are reminded of our need of Christ. In the gospel we find the amazing grace that Jesus came to share with all.

John uses slightly different words, reminding us that the law came through Moses and that grace and truth come through Jesus Christ. They are interlocking pieces of a puzzle. One without the other is a hollow faith. It is the wretched sinner who truly knows the need of grace. Undeserved favor is the sweetest of life's gifts. It is also one of the most difficult to receive. We often think, "what can I do to deserve this?" Nothing. It is amazingly given by God, whose very being is love, poured out upon a world of wretches—like me, like you.

It was not a human*ish* life that Jesus lived among us. His was a life that knew firsthand the wretchedness of human illness and pain. He touched the leper, slaked the Samaritan woman's thirst, ate with sinners, wept at the death of Lazarus. Jesus knew what it meant to be deep in the flesh of all of humanity's experiences. In his dying and rising, he shares with us the power of grace unbounded. He invites us into the sweet sound of that amazing grace.

## Prayer

Lord Jesus, may your amazing grace fill me and sustain me. Amen.

### John 1:18

No one has ever seen God. It is God the only Son, who is close to the Father's heart, who has made him known.

### To ponder

I saw the throng, so deeply separate,
Fed at one only board—
The devout people, moved, intent, elate,
And the devoted Lord.
— Alice Meynell, "A General Communion"

### More than a glimpse

The thought of seeing God is both thrilling and terrifying. Moses and the prophets either hid their faces from God or were so overcome by God's presence that they fell to the ground in awe. Yet to have that opportunity to see God face-to-face has its thrilling aspects too. Imagine the conversation at the water cooler: *"Yep. I saw God last night. It was really something."*

Perhaps we haven't had the chance for those water-cooler bragging rights because we look for God in the wrong places. John wants us to know that God is found in relationships. God is best seen in Jesus, who is close to God's heart, who has made God known.

Alice Meynell encourages us to see God in the throng. When we gather at the Lord's table we have the clearest vision possible of God. God is visible in the gathered community: "moved, intent, elate." God is equally visible to us through water and the Spirit in holy baptism, and beautifully audible to us in the Word proclaimed.

The relationships that the Word-made-flesh made while on earth are a glimpse of the God that we have yet to fully see. As we share Christ in the relationships that we form and nurture, we allow the world around us to catch more than a glimpse of the God that it may not yet have seen but can surely know.

## Prayer

Lord Jesus Christ, in all that we say and do, may our lives witness to you. We are grateful that you have chosen to become fully seen and known. Make us bold to share your presence with a world in need. Amen.

## John 1:29

The next day [John the Baptist] saw Jesus coming toward him and declared, "Here is the Lamb of God who takes away the sin of the world!"

## To ponder

Lamb of God, you take away the sin of the world, have mercy on us.—Traditional eucharistic prayer

## Meekness and might

"Lamb of God, you take away the sin of the world, have mercy on us." This brief, familiar phrase goes from meek (Lamb of God) to mighty (taking away the sin of the world) and returns to meek (have mercy on us).

From the beginning of his gospel, John wants us to know about these paradoxical characteristics of Jesus. He is as meek as a lamb. But in Christ's meekness is power. It is power sufficient to take away the sin of the world. There will be nineteen chapters before we see that meekness and power harmonize perfectly on the cross. In each encounter until then, John will be lifting up the cosmic Christ as the one who balances meekness and might.

We often eschew meekness. These days are all about "finding your voice," and "claiming your power." Those are both significant activities for finding one's way in today's world, especially in a world as complicated and diverse as ours. But claiming one's voice and finding one's power is best done as Christ would do it, in balance with meekness. We were created to share our voice and our power with one another, even as Christ shared his holy life with us. To do so with meekness brings an added blessing and, surprisingly, added strength.

From creation to the cross in John's gospel, the Lamb of God makes a way through our lives and into our hearts with a mercy that mutates into might. It is mercy forged in the fire of boundless compassion and perfected in the cross and resurrection.

## Prayer

Lord Jesus Christ, teach us to balance meekness and might in our lives. Give us courage to speak up for the sake of others, and meekness that bears witness to your self-giving love for us. Amen.

### John 1:32-34

John testified, "I saw the Spirit descending from heaven like a dove, and it remained on him. I myself did not know him, but the one who sent me to baptize with water said to me, 'He on whom you see the Spirit descend and remain is the one who baptizes with the Holy Spirit.' And I myself have seen and have testified that this is the Son of God."

### To ponder

Baptism is not simply plain water. Instead, it is water used according to God's command and connected with God's Word.
—Martin Luther, *Luther's Small Catechism*

## With all our hearts

John the Baptist's testimony makes the baptismal connection of water, Spirit, and the body of Christ. Connecting water, Spirit, and Christ is not merely a theological technicality. These associations remind us that baptism is a gift given by God, empowered by the Spirit, and belonging to all.

The Spirit's work is not in *my* heart, but in *our* hearts. The Spirit does not live in the heart of a lone believer, but in the hearts of all. Baptism belongs to the community, benefits the community, and is practiced in community. These aren't mere theological technicalities either, but the very essence of what it means to be the baptized people of God.

No one can run a food bank by themselves, at least not for long. No one can do all the things to keep a congregation healthy. Working together, we gather funds to eradicate hunger. United with others, we pool our wisdom, physical strength, or imaginations to plant community gardens or advocate for justice.

Through the Spirit, in the body of Christ, the Word is proclaimed and the miracle of Christian community is formed. In that Spirit-filled community, the risen Christ lives.

## Prayer

O Holy Spirit, enter in and dwell in all our hearts. Amen.

## John 1:35-39

The next day John again was standing with two of his disciples, and as he watched Jesus walk by, he exclaimed, "Look, here is the Lamb of God!" The two disciples heard him say this, and they followed Jesus. When Jesus turned and saw them following, he said to them, "What are you looking for?" They said to him, "Rabbi," (which translated means Teacher), "where are you staying?" He said to them, "Come and see."

## To ponder

"Come and see" is the simplest method to get to know a situation. It is the most honest test of every message, because, in order to know, we need to encounter.—Pope Francis, "Jesus' Invitation to 'Come and See'"

## Rabbi Jesus

I doubt that when Jesus invited the two disciples of John to "come and see" that he was inviting them to see his room. Instead the writer of the gospel hopes that all of us will "come and see" Jesus' journey and find what we are looking for.

When these disciples call Jesus "Rabbi" they are recognizing his gifts as a teacher. Rabbis, then and now, are those whose work immerses them in the word of God. They lead others to encounter that word in everyday events.

In this recognition of Jesus as "Rabbi" in chapter 1, John's gospel pulls us forward to Mary's recognition of Jesus as "Rabbi" at the empty tomb in chapter 20. Between these two bookends, the Rabbi Jesus will show countless followers where to find meaning, purpose, and direction for their lives. In feeding the multitudes, curing the sick, challenging the authorities, and preaching good news, Jesus is the consummate teacher. He shows followers, then and now, where to look, but not necessarily what to see. In that way he is the best of all teachers, one who says, "come and see"— *come and see for yourself.*

## Prayer

Gracious, loving teacher, lead me in paths of righteousness to see for myself the wonders of God. Amen.

## February 28

### John 1:42

[Andrew] brought Simon to Jesus, who looked at him and said, "You are Simon, son of John. You are to be called Cephas" (which is translated Peter).

### To ponder

What's in a name? That which we call a rose
By any other name would smell as sweet.
—William Shakespeare, *Romeo and Juliet*

### No other name

Within the course of one verse, Peter is referred to by three different names: Simon, Cephas, and Peter. If you add "son of John" and "the Rock," both implied, the count is five.

16

"What's in a name?" has resonated through the ages. Would Roger have become a different adult had he been named Alan? Is Jessica the woman she's become because she was not Alicia? Impossible to know.

We do know that Peter remains enigmatic in John's gospel to the very end. The strong rock who declares allegiance after the feeding of thousands is quite different from the one who later denies any knowledge of Jesus.

We also are complex, enigmatic people. The confident executive is seen differently when tenderly tucking her child into bed. A person dealing with homelessness has a history, a family, and hopes and dreams.

Of all the names one might receive, the one that means the most is the one given in baptism: child of God. Are you grumpy today? You are still a child of God. Are you celebrating a victory, personal or professional? Your baptism remains, as does your name: child of God. Whether you are having a Simon, a Cephas, or a Peter sort of day, you will always be a child of God. Could any other name sound as sweet?

## Prayer

Gracious God, thank you for making me your child in holy baptism. Be with me in this Lenten journey, that I may see myself more fully as a child of God. Amen.

### John 2:1-3, 5-7

There was a wedding in Cana of Galilee, and the mother of Jesus was there. Jesus and his disciples had also been invited to the wedding. When the wine gave out, the mother of Jesus said to him, "They have no wine." . . . His mother said to the servants, "Do whatever he tells you." Now standing there were six stone water jars. . . . "Jesus said to them, "Fill the jars with water." And they filled them up to the brim.

### To ponder

RSVP abbr [F *répondez s'il vous plaît*]: please reply.
—*Merriam-Webster's Collegiate Dictionary*

## Jesus just shows up

These days, the favor of a reply to an invitation often seems quaint. "If I decide to show up, I'll text you on the way"—that seems more like the present norm.

Did Jesus offer the favor of a reply? Something tells me that he just showed up. Apparently there were more guests than anticipated, because the wine ran out. It's also likely that Jesus just showed up, because that's what Jesus seems to do. There is a need, and he's mysteriously present. Sometimes we don't recognize his presence until afterward, but in retrospect we see that he was with us all along.

By coming into the world to live among us, Jesus has already given us a reply. He is coming. He is here. We can expect him to just show up.

The wedding couple was wise to invite Jesus to their celebration. His presence provided them with an unexpected gift of great quantity and quality. It would last them well into their first weeks and months of married life.

Jesus' presence in our world fills creation to the brim with new possibilities. And like the couple in this story, we can expect to be surprised by what his presence has to offer to us, and just how much his being among us changes things.

## Prayer

Gracious guest, be with us in our lives each day. Thank you for wedding yourself to us by becoming flesh and living among us, full of grace and truth. Amen.

## March 2

### John 2:10-11

[The steward said to the bridegroom,] "Everyone serves the good wine first. . . . But you have kept the good wine until now." Jesus did this, the first of his signs, in Cana of Galilee, and revealed his glory.

### To ponder

We give you thanks, O God, for in the beginning your Spirit moved over the waters and by your living Word you created the world, calling forth life in which you took delight.—"Holy Baptism," ELW

## A taste of new creation

In John's gospel, Jesus' ministry begins with this wonderful water story, "the first of his signs." It is a lovely parallel to the creation stories in Genesis 1 and the one at the start of this gospel ("In the beginning was the Word . . ."). As in Genesis, God's creative power brings the unexpected out of the water's dark depths, this time from water set aside for the Jewish rite of purification.

This water story is the beginning of John's larger story of the new creation. With each of the successive signs that he recounts, the evangelist will open our eyes to the marvel of Jesus' life, ministry, death, and resurrection. Each is a glimpse into the renewal of the creation that sin has left in ruin. Each glimpse shows us Christ's conviction to purify what we have destroyed.

Christ welcomes us into this new creation in baptism. There, also through water, we are given new life. Through baptism, by water and the Spirit, we are joined to the one who has overcome death itself.

Like the wine served at Cana in Galilee, the Gospel of John saves the best for last. From the cross, Jesus will proclaim, "It is finished." With those words, just as with the Creator's words in Eden, the new creation is begun. The best is saved for last. In the beginning was the Word. In the end is the Word as well. From the cross Christ calls all to new life, in which he takes delight.

## Prayer

We give you thanks for our baptism into Christ. Thank you for making us children of the new creation. Amen.

## March 3

### John 2:14-15

In the temple [Jesus] found people selling cattle, sheep, and doves, and the money changers seated at their tables. Making a whip of cords, he drove all of them out of the temple, both the sheep and the cattle. He also poured out the coins of the money changers and overturned their tables.

### To ponder

Come to your Temple here with liberation
And overturn these tables of exchange
Restore in me my lost imagination
Begin in me, for good, the pure change.
—Malcolm Guite, "Cleansing the Temple"

## Quite upsetting

There is something about having tables overturned that seems just right as Jesus visits Jerusalem for the first time. Yet this is a troubling image for most people. We'd rather think of Jesus as the kind and gentle healer. We are not sure to do with a Savior who gets angry enough to engage in violent protest.

As the gospel proceeds, it will be a story of Jesus overturning more than tables. He will overturn expectations, policies, and ways of life. He will challenge Nicodemus to think about being born again. He will stretch the imagination of thousands by feeding them from a few loaves and fish. He will send men away frustrated as they accuse a woman of adultery. Christ will overturn the expectations of two sisters as he raises their brother Lazarus from the dead. This upsets the natural order of creation, of which his own resurrection will be the keystone. He offers himself not in anger but in self-giving love, and our sins are driven out like so many money changers with their sheep and cattle.

By water and the Spirit, we are joined in baptism to this set of unruly expectations of life in Christ. Jesus invites us to overturn our lives of selfish greed and join him instead in a life like his. In baptismal dying and rising he begins in us "for good, the pure change."

## Prayer

Lord Jesus, help us to see in you the courage to overturn the things that are self-serving, and to freely give ourselves for the good of others. Amen.

## March 4

### John 2:19, 22

Jesus [said], "Destroy this temple, and in three days I will raise it up." . . . After he was raised from the dead, his disciples remembered that he had said this; and they believed the scripture and the word that Jesus had spoken.

### To ponder

Built on a rock the church shall stand,
even when steeples are falling.
—"Built on a rock," ELW 652

### Living stones

Who could have expected those around Jesus to comprehend that by *temple* he meant his body? It's even easier to understand their confusion with sheep, cattle, and doves on the loose. The money changers were standing in disbelief near their overturned tables.

We make a similar mistake, even in less nerve-wracking times. Someone mentions *church*, and we think bricks and stained glass—or, more recently, Zoom meetings or live-stream worship. It takes some doing to get us from thinking church is the building to *being* the living body of Christ, serving in the world.

Clearly this is what Jesus means, and what John wants to amplify early in his gospel. Jesus is not interested in temples, if by temples one means places of stagnant, self-serving institutional preservation. Jesus is about the power of God active in the world. Christ's is power that brings new, everlasting life out of death.

We read: "After he was raised from the dead, the disciples remembered. . . ." John wants us to get out in front of the message and remember that the church is not a building, nor was that temple. The only thing that can make a lasting difference in the lives of people is the body of Christ actively serving a world in need. Lent calls us as we prepare to be the real, living, transformative power of Jesus in the world.

## Prayer

O Risen One, help us fulfill our baptismal call to bring your living mercy into the world. Renew us for the task, and unite us as one body in your love. Amen.

## John 3:1-2

Now there was a Pharisee named Nicodemus, a leader of the Jews. He came to Jesus by night and said to him, "Rabbi, we know that you are a teacher who has come from God; for no one can do these signs that you do apart from the presence of God."

## To ponder

The true meaning of existence is disclosed in moments of living in the presence of God.—Abraham Joshua Heschel, *God in Search of Man*

## Shining in the night

Nicodemus comes to Jesus by night, perhaps a sign of his fear of being associated with Jesus, or a symbol of him not yet fully seeing God in Christ. Night could also be the realm where the light of Christ shines most brightly, so Nicodemus is able to see what he most needs but could not see before. He sees that the presence of God is intimately connected to Jesus. He might not know why or how. But Nicodemus knows God's presence must be acting in and through Jesus because where God's presence is, goodness happens.

It might be that sometimes, when it *seems* there is little light shining in the world, the goodness of God in Christ is in fact shining through more brightly. It shines through in the good deeds done in Jesus' name. It shines through in unexpected healing and extravagant grace. It shines through whatever keeps us in fear or doubt.

Look for all the ways the light of Christ is shining in this world, especially when we all need it most.

## Prayer

Your presence, Holy One, fills our lives in the day and in the night. Give us faith to know you are with us in all times. In the shining name of Jesus. Amen.

## March 6

### John 3:3-4

Jesus answered him, "Very truly, I tell you, no one can see the kingdom of God without being born from above." Nicodemus said to him, "How can anyone be born after having grown old? Can one enter a second time into the mother's womb and be born?"

### To ponder

Let this season be springtime of the soul,
time to be renewed, broken hearts made whole.
Jesus in our hearts; walk toward Easter's goal.
Let this season be springtime of the soul.
—Rusty Edwards, "Let This Season Be"

## Is it too late?

Nicodemus is confused by Jesus' language. Perhaps we are too. Being born from above? How does that happen? But Nicodemus may be more confused by something else, as might we: At some point, isn't it too late?

The old saying says you can't teach an old dog new tricks. Why? Well, they are old, and set in their ways, and no longer eager to please. Of course, it isn't exactly true, either. Old dogs can learn new tricks, but in a different way from pups.

What about us? Is it too late? If we are feeling old and tired, maybe we don't want any kind of new life Jesus is offering. Maybe we think we have come along as far as we can in learning to love and give and serve. We might feel like we have failed too often or fallen too far.

We may think it is too late, but Jesus clearly does not. His odd language about being born from above, born from water and wind, is meant to engage our imaginations to the point that we trust it is never too late. We too can become new in God's grace. We too can be born again and again and again as we live in our baptismal covenant every day.

## Prayer

God of new things, give me faith to trust every day that you make a new me and a new world possible. Help me step into that newness with gratitude and joy. Amen.

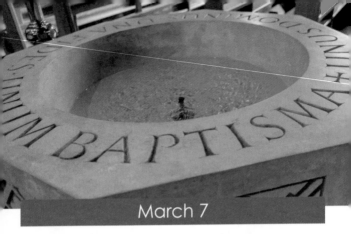

## March 7

### John 3:5-6

Jesus answered, "Very truly, I tell you, no one can enter the kingdom of God without being born of water and Spirit. What is born of the flesh is flesh, and what is born of the Spirit is spirit."

### To ponder

Those in whom the Spirit comes to live are God's new Temple. They are, individually and corporately, places where heaven and earth meet.—N. T. Wright, *Simply Christian*

## Flesh and Spirit

"What is born of the flesh is flesh." Jesus is referring here not simply to being born as a physical body from a physical body. He means that humans are born into a reality where they are more oriented toward their own goals and concerns than God's. "Flesh" in this sense is when we live out of our small, faulty human perspective, rather than trusting and living in the world filled by the God of love revealed in Jesus.

What is born of flesh is flesh. Isn't that us? We are born of human bodies and wills. We live with human-centered goals. Yes, we are that. But we are also much more because of Christ. We are born into a new life by the water and Spirit poured on us in baptism. We are reoriented toward God's love as the center of our life and concern.

We are born of flesh and Spirit. Perhaps we need to see both of those in ourselves. And then we can truly live by grace, knowing that our whole selves are created by, loved by, and accepted by God. When the gift of the Spirit is at work in us, flesh and Spirit, heaven and earth, meet together.

## Prayer

Spirit of new life, keep us centered in God's love revealed in Jesus. Empower us to love as we are loved. Amen.

## March 8

### John 3:7-8

[Jesus said,] "Do not be astonished that I said to you, 'You must be born from above.' The wind blows where it chooses, and you hear the sound of it, but you do not know where it comes from or where it goes. So it is with everyone who is born of the Spirit."

### To ponder

I need only to let faith in all its freedom exercise its power and dominion. Indeed, this is the priceless power and freedom of the Christian.—Martin Luther, *The Freedom of a Christian*

## As free as wind and water

How do you describe your life as a baptized person of faith? Forgiven? Loved? Included? All of those are certainly true. But Jesus says something else when he emphasizes "being born of water and Spirit" (John 3:5). He is pointing us to a life of freedom.

The biblical word for "Spirit" is the same as the word for "wind" in both Old and New Testaments. It's an appropriate metaphor. The Spirit moves mysteriously and freely like the wind. It cannot be controlled or contained. You can only allow yourself to be carried along with it.

The same is true for water, which Jesus also uses to describe the life of freedom lived by faith. Water flows freely. And like someone in a river, you can go with the flow, but you can't push it along. Many water parks include a ride often called a "lazy river." It is a circular channel of water with a flow created by pumps. The joy of the ride is floating along with the water wherever and however fast it takes you and everyone around you.

Nicodemus is so far confused by his conversation with Jesus. But we need not judge him harshly. Jesus is nudging him toward the faith that connects him to God. Nicodemus can only get there by being carried along by the grace of God, just like us.

## Prayer

Spirit of freedom, carry us along by your love. In Jesus' name, amen.

## John 3:14-15

[Jesus said,] "And just as Moses lifted up the serpent in the wilderness, so must the Son of Man be lifted up, that whoever believes in him may have eternal life."

## To ponder

Our goal is to ascertain the existence of a Being to whom we may confess our sins, of a God who loves, of a God who is not above concern with our inquiry and search for him; a father, not an absolute. —Abraham Joshua Heschel, *God in Search of Man*

## Reflecting the truth

Mirrors can be a blessing or a curse. They can show us at our best, like when we're dressed up to go to a special occasion, hair and makeup and jewelry just right. Mirrors can also show us at our worst. No one likes to see themselves in the mirror when they are sick. It's not a pretty sight.

Moses lifted up the serpent in the wilderness to be a mirror to the people. They had rejected God's guidance, and God judged them by sending poisonous snakes. But that wasn't the end of it. God then sent healing for the poison. But the only way for the healing to work was to see the poison of their own failed ways.

Jesus is lifted up on the cross for the same reason Moses lifted up the serpent. The crucified Jesus is a mirror that shows us we are sick, that human ways can be ugly, that sin is real. The cross is humanity at its worst. But to look on the cross and see God's presence in Christ is also to see healing. Grace meets ugliness. Love conquers hate. Seeing God fully revealed in the humility and suffering of Jesus is to know God in an entirely new way, a way that heals and sets free.

## Prayer

O God, give us courage to look at ourselves and see where we have strayed from your ways. Heal us by your grace so we may love. Amen.

## March 10

### John 3:16

[Jesus said,] "For God so loved the world that he gave his only Son, so that everyone who believes in him may not perish but may have eternal life."

### To ponder

Oh, love, how deep, how broad, how high,
beyond all thought and fantasy,
that God, the Son of God, should take
our mortal form for mortals' sake!
—"Oh, love, how deep," ELW 322

## Swimming or diving

If you're planning on swimming laps in a pool, the length of the pool determines how many laps you need to complete. If it is too short, you would constantly be flipping around. If it is too long, you might never get a needed break swimming from one end to the other.

If you're wanting to dive into a pool, the depth determines the height you can dive from. If a pool is too shallow, diving would be unsafe above a certain height. But when a pool is deep and safe, you can jump and free fall and twist and splash.

When Jesus speaks about eternal life, we often think he means the length of life. That assumes we are always going to exist within the boundaries of time. But God is outside of time, so eternal life must mean something else.

Eternal life means a life of depth. It means knowing that we are always caught by the buoyant waters of God's grace. It means living in a profound sense of all-embracing love, whether here and now, or in the mystery of life after death. Eternal life is about the depth of life we live in God through Christ—and it is deep.

When we live with faith in God's unending love for us and the whole world, we are empowered to dive into life with God and know we are safe.

## Prayer

God of love, hold me in your eternal embrace now and beyond time. Amen.

## March 11

### John 3:17

[Jesus said,] "Indeed, God did not send the Son into the world to condemn the world, but in order that the world might be saved through him."

### To ponder

The real scandal of the gospel is this: humanity's salvation is revealed in the cross of the condemned criminal Jesus, and humanity's salvation is available only through our solidarity with the crucified people in our midst.—James Cone, *The Cross and the Lynching Tree*

## Worth saving

Imagine you own a house. It's run down. It needs foundation work, roof work, painting, and more. It's a lot of work and probably a great expense to fix it, but you've decided it's worth it. Then your municipality decides the house is too far gone and condemns it. Someone else offers to buy your house, calling it a "tear-down" and plans to replace it with something new. You would probably be shocked that the house you wanted to save others thought was beyond fixing. You thought it was a keeper.

That same shock should come to people of faith when we hear someone claim that God condemns the world or individuals. It implies that the world or a particular person is too far gone, is beyond saving or repair. It assumes that tearing down—destroying—is the only path forward.

Jesus brings us a different way. Jesus brings us the way of repairing, fixing, saving what is already precious in God's sight: the world, and all the individuals in it. There are no tear-down persons, and there's no condemning the world like giving up on a dilapidated house. The good news comes from the one the world condemned, but God resurrected. The good news comes for all who face condemnation in this world.

God's love says: you also are worth it. You're a keeper.

## Prayer

O God, help us to trust in your grace for us and others. Keep us from thinking anyone is beyond your love. For Jesus' sake. Amen.

## March 12 / Lent 3

### John 4:7, 9-10

A Samaritan woman came to draw water, and Jesus said to her, "Give me a drink." . . . The Samaritan woman said to him, "How is it that you, a Jew, ask a drink of me, a woman of Samaria?" (Jews do not share things in common with Samaritans.) Jesus answered her, "If you knew the gift of God, and who it is that is saying to you, 'Give me a drink,' you would have asked him, and he would have given you living water."

### To ponder

I'm a Vietnam veteran, I did two tours in the jungle . . . and I came home from that. So I don't pass the flowers up; I smell them. A lot of guys used to try to rush to get done, and maybe get back to the garage and hang out a little bit. And that's OK. Everybody has their own way. But I always like the street; I always like talking to the people.—Angelo Bruno, sanitation worker, in *Callings*

## God in the everyday

Going to the well to draw water was a simple, everyday chore. Like collecting the trash on the street, it must be done, over and over again, every day. Life-giving grace appears in the everyday moment in simple conversations with others.

Sometimes we long for amazing and outstanding moments to encounter God and rush past the small glimmers of grace in the everyday tasks of life. There is blessedness in greeting strangers and sharing a cup of water in the heat of the day. Jesus met the woman in her everyday chore with a simple request. In that moment, what she had to offer in drawing water became the very thing that carried the grace of God.

## Prayer

God of everyday life, in our daily tasks of living, show us your presence and grace. Meet us in the mundane, training our hearts to wonder at your life-giving hope in Jesus Christ. Amen.

## March 13

### John 4:11-14

The woman said to [Jesus], "Sir, you have no bucket, and the well
is deep. Where do you get that living water? Are you greater than
our ancestor Jacob, who gave us the well, and with his sons and
his flocks drank from it?" Jesus said to her, "Everyone who drinks
of this water will be thirsty again, but those who drink of the
water that I will give them will never be thirsty. The water that
I will give will become in them a spring of water gushing up to
eternal life."

### To ponder

It's a delightful world out there, and I think we ought to notice.
God noticed, at the end of each day of creation, what a lovely

world it was: "And God saw that it was good." I think God intends for us just such delight. —Lee Hull Moses, *More than Enough*

## God's delight

On the one hand, it was just a well that gave water to drink for generations. On the other hand, it was a marvel of delight and provision: a well that provided water to drink for generations. The woman knew that the well had provided water to quench physical thirst for decades.

In the beginning, Genesis tells us, God moved over the waters and called forth life into being. The waters that sustained life began before our lives even began. The waters connect us and flow through us. The woman's encounter with Jesus moved her from observation about daily life and family history into a larger reality beyond her experience. I imagine that she looked at the water differently as it transformed in her eyes from daily provision into eternal hope. Jesus proclaims God's delight and abundance in creation.

## Prayer

God of life, your creation delights and sustains us with abundance and constancy. Help us to notice the ways you provide for all through Jesus Christ, our Lord. Amen.

## John 4:15-19

The woman said to [Jesus], "Sir, give me this water, so that I may never be thirsty or have to keep coming here to draw water." Jesus said to her, "Go, call your husband, and come back." The woman answered him, "I have no husband." Jesus said to her, "You are right in saying, 'I have no husband'; for you have had five husbands, and the one you have now is not your husband." . . . The woman said to him, "Sir, I see that you are a prophet."

## To ponder

Many Christians are unthinkably horrified when a real sinner is suddenly discovered among the righteous. So we remain alone in our sin, living in lies and hypocrisy. The fact is that we are sinners!—Dietrich Bonhoeffer, *Life Together*

## Community connection

She never lied, she simply confessed one thing without confessing everything. Perhaps she was guarded and cautious, not feeling safe enough to share the story of her life with a stranger, even though the details of her life were certainly known to the community. Jesus saw the truth—not just about the woman but about everyone. After all, she was not alone in her story; she had five husbands and another companion. The woman called Jesus a prophet, realizing that he saw her clearly. Jesus met her in her vulnerability, building relationship and trust. Jesus loved her beyond her guardedness.

What would our community be like if we shared vulnerability with one another and recognized that we are deeply connected by the grace we all need? No one is without sin, and no one is alone in sin. Christ draws us into the place where we can let down our guard with one another. Connected by brokenness, we are healed together into grace, love, hope, and community.

## Prayer

God of grace, you know the sins and brokenness of every human being. Give us the courage to meet one another in our vulnerabilities so that we dance together in your grace through Jesus Christ, our Lord. Amen.

## March 15

### John 4:23-26

[Jesus said,] "The hour is coming, and is now here, when the true worshipers will worship the Father in spirit and truth, for the Father seeks such as these to worship him. God is spirit, and those who worship him must worship in spirit and truth." The woman said to him, "I know that Messiah is coming" (who is called Christ). "When he comes, he will proclaim all things to us." Jesus said to her, "I am he."

### To ponder

Making do reaches fruition when someone dares to imagine another possibility greater than what appears to be the reality.
—Michael Curry, *Love Is the Way*

## Greater possibilities

The woman was waiting and watching for the Messiah, poised to encounter the one who would change everything. The teachings of scripture prepared her mind and created a set of expectations, like one who reads a travel guide before experiencing the wonders of the world. One's preparation rarely fully prepares the imagination for the wonder and delight of lived experience.

Jesus proclaimed, "I am he," confirming the culmination of the woman's hope and putting an end to her faithful preparations. In that moment in the middle of everyday life, she looked into the face of the Savior, whose presence proclaims all things and changes all things. Now there was realized hope and new possibility.

The Spirit of God seeks us out with living encounters of God that cause our preparations to fade into greater possibilities than we could ever imagine. We dare to go about our daily lives and faithful worship with the promise that God will bring new possibilities to life.

## Prayer

Loving God, love us beyond our preparations into living encounters with grace and hope through Jesus Christ, our Lord. Amen.

## March 16

### John 4:28-30, 39-42

Then the woman left her water jar and went back to the city. She said to the people, "Come and see a man who told me everything I have ever done! He cannot be the Messiah, can he?" They left the city and were on their way to him. . . . Many Samaritans from that city believed in him because of the woman's testimony. . . . So when the Samaritans came to [Jesus], they asked him to stay with them; and he stayed there two days. And many more believed because of his word. They said to the woman, "It is no longer because of what you said that we believe, for we have heard for ourselves, and we know that this is truly the Savior of the world."

## To ponder

Moments of compassion, giving, grief, and wonder shift our behavior, get inside us and change realms we might not have agreed to change.—Anne Lamott, *Hallelujah Anyway*

## Contagious hope

It's not likely that the woman had ever considered what could be changed in her life. Perhaps she longed for transformation but couldn't imagine how that might happen in her and around her.

After her encounter with Jesus' grace and compassion, something shifted inside the woman. Hope radiated through her. Her daily experience of life became the foundation of undeniable delight, amazement, and joy.

People noticed the change in the woman as she returned to the city. In the past many may have seen the woman only as fodder for gossip. Now they saw her as a bearer of God's presence and witness to the Messiah in their midst. The hope she exuded drew people to Jesus, to see and hear him for themselves.

Who drew you to Jesus? How might God use your story to draw others in?

## Prayer

Help us, O God, to encounter your love and compassion in new ways. Transform our lives and inspire us to share our stories of life and hope as we live into the grace you intend for all people through Jesus Christ, our Lord. Amen.

## John 6:5, 7-9, 11

When he looked up and saw a large crowd coming toward him, Jesus said to Philip, "Where are we to buy bread for these people to eat?" . . . Philip answered him, "Six months' wages would not buy enough bread for each of them to get a little." One of his disciples, Andrew, Simon Peter's brother, said to him, "There is a boy here who has five barley loaves and two fish. But what are they among so many people?" Jesus said, "Make the people sit down." . . . Then Jesus took the loaves, and when he had given thanks, he distributed them to those who were seated; so also the fish, as much as they wanted.

## To ponder

The bread you do not use is the bread of the hungry.... The money you keep locked away is the money of the poor. The acts of charity you do not perform are the injustices you commit.
—St. Basil the Great

## Enough

*What do I have to offer? I'm only one person; I can't possibly address or solve the world's problems!* The overwhelming needs in the world can feel paralyzing. We don't know where to even begin.

Philip and Andrew were stuck in a mindset that saw only scarcity. Limited resources would not be enough with such a large crowd. But what is *enough?* The simple offering of a child became enough in the hands of an abundant, extravagant God.

What would it look like to give thanks for what we have, the gifts we bring to the table, and how God has empowered us? To embrace who God created us to be and be blessed in that knowledge? Might we then allow ourselves to be generous and broken open for a world hungry and thirsty for God's grace?

## Prayer

Holy One, give me bold courage to trust that it *is* enough, to trust that *I* am enough in your precious grace. Amen.

## March 18

### John 6:48-51

[Jesus said,] "I am the bread of life. Your ancestors ate the manna in the wilderness, and they died. This is the bread that comes down from heaven, so that one may eat of it and not die. I am the living bread that came down from heaven. Whoever eats of this bread will live forever; and the bread that I will give for the life of the world is my flesh."

### To ponder

Breathe in the love of God,
Let it fill you with grace and mercy.
Breathe in the life of God,

Let it empower you with truth and justice.
Breathe in the peace of God,
Let it sustain you with faith and hope.
—Christine Sine, "Prayers for the Journey"

## A slice of life

Until I lived in Germany, I didn't really understand the power of delicious bread. Bakeries were everywhere and fresh bread was a *thing*! Crusty loaves that crackled and sang as you sliced through them. Rolls perfect for slathering on rich butter and sweet jams. Dense multigrain slices layered with savory cheeses and salty slices of cured meats. I miss the bread that made each day a delightful discovery of new tantalizing combinations of carbs and toppings, and a reminder to celebrate the little, daily joys in life.

But the more lasting sustenance during my time there was the mystery of overflowing love I experienced while hearing about Jesus in a chilly Lutheran church early on Sunday mornings. It was in the words I wrestled with and wanted to better understand as I slowly read through the Bible for the first time. What sustained me through questions and doubts was Christ's unconditional welcome and love. I learned to taste and see that God is good, as God-given curiosity and hunger to learn more drew me more fully into relationship with the living bread of life.

## Prayer

Lord Jesus, you sustain us with your love. Thanks be to God! Amen.

## March 19 / Lent 4

### John 9:1, 6-9

As [Jesus] walked along, he saw a man blind from birth. . . .
[Jesus] spat on the ground and made mud with the saliva and
spread the mud on the man's eyes, saying to him, "Go, wash in the
pool of Siloam" (which means Sent). Then he went and washed
and came back able to see. The neighbors and those who had seen
him before as a beggar began to ask, "Is this not the man who
used to sit and beg?" Some were saying, "It is he." Others were
saying, "No, but it is someone like him." He kept saying, "I am the
man."

### To ponder

The Word became flesh to communicate to us human beings
caught in the mud, the pain, the fears and the brokenness of exis-

tence, the life, the joy, the communion, the ecstatic gift of love that is the source of all love and life and unity in our universe and that is the very life of God.—Jean Vanier, in *Lives that Made a Difference*

## Through the mud

In Genesis God forms people as earth-creatures and breathes life into them. In today's scripture text, Jesus spits and makes mud, bringing vision through the muck of everyday life. The man's sight is restored, but his name is dragged through the mud when people with limited vision question him, make assumptions, and refuse to believe him. "Those who had seen him before as a beggar" had difficulty grasping the man's good news.

We all slog through mud—the challenges, sorrows, and pains of life. Truth be told, we often wallow in the mud and, like the onlookers in this story, refuse to listen, to be challenged, or to remain open to God's perspective.

In Jesus, God incarnate, God blesses the dust of the earth—our humble, human lives—and redeems those moments when we are stuck in the mud. Do we have eyes to see the blessing in the mundane?

## Prayer

Jesus, grant us vision to see clearly how you sanctify humble, daily life. Amen.

## John 9:13-16

[People] brought to the Pharisees the man who had formerly been blind. Now it was a sabbath day when Jesus made the mud and opened his eyes. Then the Pharisees also began to ask him how he had received his sight. He said to them, "He put mud on my eyes. Then I washed, and now I see." Some of the Pharisees said, "This man is not from God, for he does not observe the sabbath." But others said, "How can a man who is a sinner perform such signs?"

## To ponder

Sabbath is that uncluttered time and space in which we can distance ourselves from our own activities enough to see what God is doing.—Eugene Peterson, in *The Pastor's Guide to Personal Spiritual Formation*

## Rest to receive

During the pandemic many began working from home, and the lines between work and home life blurred. Now the office was in a space previously used for relaxation, and Zoom meetings could be held any time. Without regular rhythms of work and play, activity and rest, time seemed both to evaporate and to last forever.

Some people complained that Jesus did not keep the sabbath when he restored sight in the man born blind. Keeping sabbath is one of the commandments, but it's easy to forget *why* it is a command. Sabbath is a time to rest, knowing God is active, and to be in awe of what God is doing. Sabbath is a time to release control, recognizing that work will always be there. This is not just a Pharisee issue. Think about how many "shoulds" pop up as you try to worship or pray—to-do lists, errands that need to be run, and so on. Sabbath is a time God *gifts* to us for the healing of mind, body, and spirit as we keep company with God.

## Prayer

God of the sabbath, help me to let go of unhealthy habits of overwork so I may delight and rest in you. Amen.

## March 21

### John 9:18-21

[Others] did not believe that he had been blind and had received his sight until they called the parents of the man who had received his sight and asked them, "Is this your son, who you say was born blind? How then does he now see?" His parents answered, "We know that this is our son, and that he was born blind; but we do not know how it is that now he sees, nor do we know who opened his eyes. Ask him; he is of age. He will speak for himself."

### To ponder

Develop enough courage so that you can stand up for yourself and then stand up for somebody else.—Maya Angelou, in *Rainbow in the Cloud*

## Finding courage

John's gospel seems to capture the societal pressure and fear experienced by the man's parents. They must have been excited to witness their son's joy, but didn't want to make statements inviting the ire of others who were confounded or agitated by what Jesus had done. So they took a step back, stuck to the facts, and allowed their son to speak for himself. I want them to have their son's back, show courage, and tell the community to stop harassing their son and rejoice at the good news, but I also know that, despite our best intentions, we sometimes allow fear to silence us.

Who gives you courage to speak truth? To stand up to bullies, to stop gossip or misinformation? Others couldn't or wouldn't believe the man until they heard his parents' scant testimony. Might even our feeble attempts to advocate or speak truth help others find their courage?

## Prayer

Holy One, give me courage to advocate and stand up for others. Amen.

## March 22

### John 9:24-25, 32-34

So for the second time [the people] called the man who had been blind, and they said to him, "Give glory to God! We know that this man is a sinner." He answered, "I do not know whether he is a sinner. One thing I do know, that though I was blind, now I see. . . . Never since the world began has it been heard that anyone opened the eyes of a person born blind. If this man were not from God, he could do nothing." They answered him, "You were born entirely in sins, and are you trying to teach us?" And they drove him out.

### To ponder

The way we see things is affected by what we know or what we believe.—John Berger, in "Ways of Seeing"

## Seeing with the heart

How often do we discount something simply because it comes from unexpected people and places? The man born blind had a heart open to receiving God as God showed up in his life. He didn't get caught up in outward appearances, rules, or regulations, or what was a right or wrong way for God to be, act, or appear. But the man told others what had happened during his encounter with Jesus, and it was difficult for them to believe him.

God has been present and taught me through the beauty and intricacies of creation. When I'm in my own head, worried or fretting about things, there have been occasions when squirrels chasing each other have reminded me not to take myself so seriously. They've gently helped me loosen up and return to a more positive and grateful perspective.

God is always inviting us into the expansive mystery and playfulness of mercy and grace. How is God appearing to you in mysterious and startling ways during this Lenten season?

## Prayer

God of mystery, open my heart to receive your grace, even in unexpected, baffling, and playful ways. Amen.

## March 23

### John 9:35-38

Jesus heard that they had driven [the man] out, and when he found him, he said, "Do you believe in the Son of Man?" He answered, "And who is he, sir? Tell me, so that I may believe in him." Jesus said to him, "You have seen him, and the one speaking with you is he." He said, "Lord, I believe." And he worshiped him.

### To ponder

Love all God's creation, the whole and every grain of sand in it. Love every leaf, every ray of God's light. Love the animals, love the plants, love everything. If you love everything, you will perceive the divine mystery in things. Once you perceive it, you will begin to comprehend it better every day.—Fyodor Dostoevsky, *The Brothers Karamazov*

## Seen and unseen

This man wanted and was ready to believe. Imagine Jesus smiling as he told this beloved child of God, "You have seen [the Son of Man], and the one speaking with you is he." Although the man still had mud on his eyes when Jesus appears to have left him, he saw and recognized Jesus without needing physical sight. He could see beyond what others with 20/20 vision perceived.

As we continue our Lenten journey, ask the Holy Spirit to reveal to you the God who seeks you out, even in this moment. The Spirit given to us in baptism teaches us to "perceive the divine mystery" over a lifetime. Where do you experience hesitation or disbelief in your relationship with the triune God? Ask God for the grace to proclaim "Lord, I believe" with our ancestor, the man who perceived what could only be seen with the eyes of faith.

## Prayer

Jesus, thank you for seeking out every one of us. I believe. Help my unbelief. Amen.

## March 24

### John 10:7-11

Jesus said to them, "Very truly, I tell you, I am the gate for the sheep. All who came before me are thieves and bandits; but the sheep did not listen to them. I am the gate. Whoever enters by me will be saved, and will come in and go out and find pasture. The thief comes only to steal and kill and destroy. I came that they may have life, and have it abundantly. I am the good shepherd."

### To ponder

Christ's redemption from the sin that separates us from our whole relationship with our Creator (our "justification" before God, in Luther's language), empowers Latinas in our claim for abundant life for ourselves, our families and our communities within the oppression and marginalization that defines Latinas' life in the U.S.—Alicia Vargas, "Mujerismo and the Two Kin-Doms"

## Abundant life

It is so easy to buy the lie of scarcity: there isn't enough food to go around, not enough money, not enough time, not enough houses, not enough power, not enough (fill in the blank). When we believe that lie, it turns even the best of us into "thieves and bandits." When we have a mindset of scarcity, we seek life from more: more food, more money, more time, more power, more (fill in the blank).

The fact is that none of those things will give you life. Rather, when your focus becomes "more," which is usually "more for me and mine," you end up marginalizing your neighbor and make it more difficult for the most vulnerable to thrive.

Jesus came that we might be freed from this vicious cycle of violence and moved to participate in the abundant life that God alone provides. There is enough when we allow Jesus to be our Good Shepherd. Together may we journey in and out with Jesus to pastures where there is enough for every child of God.

## Prayer

Good Shepherd, give me eyes to see the world through the lens of your abundance. Allow me to cooperate with all your children for the sake of our mutual thriving. Amen.

## March 25

### John 10:27-28

[Jesus said,] "My sheep hear my voice. I know them, and they follow me. I give them eternal life, and they will never perish. No one will snatch them out of my hand."

### To ponder

At camp, I finally understood I am claimed by God, as a child of God, through baptism. This understanding allowed me to see that my unique heritage as a Lumbee Native American was to be celebrated. I now know that each culture also has a unique perspective to share with the church that needs to be heard. I now feel empowered as a child of God, and as a Lumbee Native American, to share my heritage and my faith, not separately but in union.—Branden Hunt, "Claimed by God through Baptism"

## Claimed by God

Something very important happens in baptism. We are claimed by God, by our parents, by godparents, by extended family and friends, by the congregation gathered, and by the whole church! We receive the message that we matter to God and the community through the promise of water and word. On top of that, we receive the promise that Jesus will never let us go. In baptism it doesn't matter what language is spoken, the color of skin, the sexual identity, the age, the ethnicity, or any other label we may cast on one another. Here the only thing that matters is that God has lovingly placed us into the hands of Jesus, just as we are.

In the scripture text we get an image of Jesus as one who holds on to us and will never let us go. We may feel like we stray away here and there, for hours, days, or even years. But even though we sometimes try our best to wriggle free from the grasp of Jesus, in the end we remain in the firm yet gentle embrace of our keeper.

## Prayer

God, I am listening for your voice. Let me hear you calling my name, that I may know you have claimed me as your own and will never let me go. Amen.

## March 26 / Lent 5

### John 11:1, 3, 6

Now a certain man was ill, Lazarus of Bethany, the village of Mary and her sister Martha. . . . So the sisters sent a message to Jesus, "Lord, he whom you love is ill." . . . After having heard that Lazarus was ill, he stayed two days longer in the place where he was.

### To ponder

We are waiting, if not for the Messiah, as such, we are waiting for the messianic moment. And the messianic moment is what each and every one of us tries to build, meaning a certain area of humanity that links us to all those who are human and, therefore, desperately trying to fight despair as humanly as possible and—I hope—with some measure of success.—Elie Wiesel, "Learning and Respect," commencement speech

## Waiting for Jesus

There is no way around it, this is a difficult text to read. Why didn't Jesus get up and go when he received Mary and Martha's message? We can say, perhaps, that Jesus was testing their faith, that Jesus knew Lazarus would come back, that this was meant for the greater good, but we are left, at this point in the Lazarus story, with pain and heartache.

I imagine you have had this question deep in your heart as well. You have found yourself praying for Jesus to show up amid a very hard situation, an illness, or even impending death. You have wondered whether God would come. The gospels of Mark and Matthew describe Jesus saying on the cross, "My God, why have you abandoned me?"

If Jesus can ask this question, surely we are free to do the same. As we wait for Jesus to appear, we remain faithful by naming the pain and calling for him to show up once more.

## Prayer

Jesus, we are waiting for you to show up. Send us your peace that surpasses all understanding, that even amid our pain, we may find your presence with us. Amen.

## John 11:17, 20-24

When Jesus arrived, he found that Lazarus had already been in the tomb four days. . . . When Martha heard that Jesus was coming, she went and met him, while Mary stayed at home. Martha said to Jesus, "Lord, if you had been here, my brother would not have died. But even now I know that God will give you whatever you ask of him." Jesus said to her, "Your brother will rise again." Martha said to him, "I know that he will rise again in the resurrection on the last day."

## To ponder

Q: Have you ever had doubts about your faith?
A: Doubts? No. Anger with God? Yes. Plenty of that. I've remonstrated with God quite frequently and said, "What the heck are

you up to? Why are you letting these oppressors get away with this injustice?" But doubting that God is good? That God is love? No.—Desmond Tutu, "10 Questions for Desmond Tutu"

## Where have you been?

Martha has a deep faith. She comes to Jesus and expresses the deep pain of losing her brother, her disappointment that Jesus didn't show up sooner, and in the same breath acknowledges God will be at work in and through Jesus. In the depths of her grief, Martha has not fallen into despair. She is still able to articulate what little hope she can muster. She doesn't know exactly what Jesus can do, but she knows that Jesus can do something.

Jesus responds with a promise, "your brother will rise again."

Martha's reply demonstrates that she doesn't quite understand what Jesus means. Jesus is promising life now, not in some distant future. When Jesus shows up, anything is possible. Healing is possible, liberation is possible, life from death is possible!

## Prayer

Gracious God, keep the flame of faith alive in my heart, even in the most difficult of circumstances. Amen.

### John 11:25-27

Jesus said to [Martha], "I am the resurrection and the life. Those who believe in me, even though they die, will live, and everyone who lives and believes in me will never die. Do you believe this?" She said to him, "Yes, Lord, I believe that you are the Messiah, the Son of God, the one coming into the world."

### To ponder

Belief initiates and guides action—or it does nothing.
—Octavia Butler, *Parable of the Sower*

## Do you believe this?

Jesus now brings this encounter with Martha to its climax. He proclaims that the promise of life is not just about the future, but it is also about the now. Jesus is the resurrection and the life right now!

In baptism we claim the promise of new life every day. Every morning we have the opportunity to choose life and life abundant.

Today I invite you into a time of meditation. Make yourself comfortable. Focus on your breath for a few moments.

Take a deep breath. This is God's breath of life. Feel it invigorating every cell in your body.

Take another deep breath. This is the Holy Spirit. Ask for direction this day. Where might God be calling you?

Take another deep breath. This is the breath of Jesus. This is resurrection and life. Where do you need new life today?

Take three more deep breaths and allow Jesus to give you life today.

## Prayer

Jesus Christ, you are the resurrection and the life. Fill me with your enlivening spirit, that I may be a vessel of your liberating love in the world. Amen.

### John 11:32-35

When Mary came where Jesus was and saw him, she knelt at his feet and said to him, "Lord, if you had been here, my brother would not have died." When Jesus saw her weeping, and the Jews who came with her also weeping, he was greatly disturbed in spirit and deeply moved. He said, "Where have you laid him?" They said to him, "Lord, come and see." Jesus began to weep.

### To ponder

Jesus' tears are an honest sharing in Mary's grief and perhaps in her anger at death, the enemy of all life. Jesus, in his most fully human moment in the Fourth Gospel, legitimates human agony in the face of death, an agony he will feel for himself. —Sandra M. Schneiders, "Death in the Community of Eternal Life"

## Jesus weeps

Jesus' encounter with Mary and the community is quite different from his conversation with Martha. Mary comes to Jesus sad, mad, broken, crying. Mary just needs Jesus to be there. So . . . Jesus doesn't say much. Jesus steps into Mary's pain and weeps.

As a young chaplain I was once called to the room of a patient who had just been told she was going to die. I had no idea what to say or do, but something deep within gave me the courage to open the door, through which I could hear gut-wrenching wailing. I stepped in, pulled up a chair and sat. The crying continued. Eventually the patient looked at me and asked, "What do you think?" I said, "I think it's okay to be feeling the way you are right now."

Jesus doesn't gloss over the tears and cries of Mary and the crowd. Jesus enters in and goes to the source of their pain. If your heart aches this day, know that Jesus weeps with you. You are not alone in your sorrow.

## Prayer

O Jesus, you weep for all who are burdened, mourning, crying, and wailing. May your tears be a balm for weary hearts. Amen.

## March 30

### John 11:38-41

Then Jesus, again greatly disturbed, came to the tomb. It was a cave, and a stone was lying against it. Jesus said, "Take away the stone." Martha, the sister of the dead man, said to him, "Lord, already there is a stench because he has been dead four days." Jesus said to her, "Did I not tell you that if you believed, you would see the glory of God?" So they took away the stone.

### To ponder

Despair, so deep it bears no name, or sorrows paralyzing cannot revoke Love's faithful claim to dwell within our dying.

The Love that called creation good all goodness still is bringing.
This Love turns death again to life and silence into singing.
—"Before the waters nourished earth," ACS 1049

## Is it too late?

Martha, the sister of Lazarus who first met Jesus and proclaimed her faith, is now compelled to ask the question, "But Jesus, isn't it too late?" After four days in a tomb, Lazarus is surely dead and his body decaying. Can any good come from opening this tomb?

We can be easily moved to judge Martha. Didn't Jesus already tell her what he was about to do? Hasn't she already confessed Jesus as Messiah? Where does this doubt come from?

Reality is, we've all been here. We've had our doubts. We've questioned whether Jesus could really breathe new life into a particular situation. And . . .

Reality is, we all have stories—or have heard stories—about times when Jesus wasn't too late, when something too far gone and better left in a tomb was miraculously brought back to life, and the "glory of God" shone. So is it too late? No, it's never too late for Jesus. Doubts may come and go, but God's liberating love will continue to pursue us, bringing peace and wholeness.

## Prayer

When I think it's too late and things are too far gone, come to me, Lord Jesus. Show me that it's not too late and breathe new life into me. Amen.

## March 31

### John 11:43-44

[Jesus] cried with a loud voice, "Lazarus, come out!" The dead man came out, his hands and feet bound with strips of cloth, and his face wrapped in a cloth. Jesus said to them, "Unbind him, and let him go."

### To ponder

God is not only with us in terms of God's presence in history on the side of the oppressed; but . . . God is in the flesh of even the "oppressed of the oppressed.". . . "God in us" presumes an already "there-ness" of God and thereby compels the church to recognize injustice against any body, most especially those bodies that defy normativity, as injustice against God.—Eboni Marshall Turman, *Toward a Womanist Ethic of Incarnation*

## Our part in an ongoing story

Jesus did it! He called out to Lazarus and brought him back to life.

Jesus is doing it! Still today he calls out to those at death's door, bringing them resurrection. He calls all marginalized individuals and communities to step out from their tombs and into new and abundant life. Every day Jesus does this work of bringing new life forward from the peripheries of society, even as he constantly tears down the walls that divide us.

Now look back at today's scripture text. It ends not when Lazarus emerges from the tomb but when Jesus calls out to the crowd to unbind and release Lazarus. He calls the people to take part in freeing Lazarus and giving him a new lease on life.

We may not see the tethers that keep people from thriving, unwittingly allowing many to remain bound by oppressive systems that benefit only the few. But every day God is calling our neighbors into liberation and new life, and it is the work of God's people to unbind them, release them, and allow new life to flourish.

## Prayer

God of restoration and new life, unbind your precious children, ensnared by cloths of inequity and shame. Empower us to take part in this liberating action in the world. Amen.

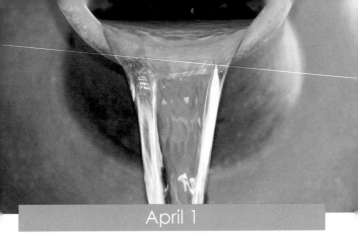

## April 1

### John 12:1, 3-5, 7

Jesus came to Bethany, the home of Lazarus, whom he had raised from the dead. . . . Mary took a pound of costly perfume made of pure nard, anointed Jesus' feet, and wiped them with her hair. . . . But Judas Iscariot, one of his disciples . . . said, "Why was this perfume not sold for three hundred denarii and the money given to the poor?" . . . Jesus said, "Leave her alone. She bought it so that she might keep it for the day of my burial."

### To ponder

Even if I knew that tomorrow the world would go to pieces, I would still plant my apple tree.—attributed to Martin Luther

## Apple trees

What would you do if you knew the world would end tomorrow? Order dessert, perhaps. Discover thankfulness. Say the words that matter to the people who matter most.

In the days before Jesus' arrest and crucifixion, few of his disciples realized that the world they knew was ending. But Mary knew. Like a hospice worker, Mary gently cared for Jesus, anointing his feet with oil and with the water of her tears. When Judas self-righteously chastised Mary for her waste, Jesus corrected him, pointing to the true purpose of her action. Mary was preparing for the end of the world.

Could Mary have meant this anointing not only for death, but also for something more? We don't know—but we do know that the world did not just end with Jesus' death. It also began anew. Like an apple seed buried in the ground, Jesus emerged from the tomb of his burial, alive and transformed: the risen Christ.

Worlds end, and new worlds begin: this is the promise of every apple seed, and the promise of resurrection. May we enter this Holy Week secure in that promise.

## Prayer

God of endings and beginnings, your Spirit carries us through every season of change. As Mary did, let us release our expectations and treasure what is true. Hold us in your love and promises. Amen.

## April 2 / Sunday of the Passion

### John 12:12-15

The great crowd that had come to the festival heard that Jesus was coming to Jerusalem. So they took branches of palm trees and went out to meet him, shouting, "Hosanna! Blessed is the one who comes in the name of the Lord—the King of Israel!" Jesus found a young donkey and sat on it; as it is written: "Do not be afraid, daughter of Zion. Look, your king is coming, sitting on a donkey's colt!"

### To ponder

Despair and hope. They travel the road to Jerusalem together, as together they travel every road we take.—Frederick Buechner, *A Room Called Remember*

## Palms to palms

How quickly the cries of "Hosanna!" turned to cries of "Crucify him!" How quickly the palm branches lifted high in the air to welcome Jesus vanished, replaced by the palms of Jesus stretched wide on the cross.

We might wonder how this could have happened. Yet human history tells this story again and again: the shift in the crowd, and fear crashing down like a wave on the shore. Even in our time, with a world of information at our fingertips, we can easily be caught up in rumors, overwhelmed by the anxiety around us, and swept along on a tide of grief and blame.

In the crowd that day, some no doubt hoped for a leader who would inspire them to rise up and fight for freedom from Roman occupation. Others feared that, because the status quo had given them wealth and power. Still others simply buckled under pressure, shouting along with the crowd because it seemed dangerous not to. And so it goes.

Yet this time there was more to the story: not only death, but resurrection. The crucified palms of Jesus became the hands of the risen Christ, stretched out to embrace the entire world in healing and redemption.

## Prayer

God of mercy, hold us and all people in the palm of your hand. Mend what is broken. Heal what is wounded. Forgive our failings. Grant us courage to walk with you, hand in hand. Amen.

## John 12:16-18

His disciples did not understand these things at first; but when Jesus was glorified, then they remembered that these things had been written of him and had been done to him. So the crowd that had been with him when he called Lazarus out of the tomb and raised him from the dead continued to testify. It was also because they heard that he had performed this sign that the crowd went to meet him.

## To ponder

God of grace and God of glory, on your people pour your power. . . . Grant us wisdom, grant us courage, for the facing of this hour, for the facing of this hour.—"God of grace and God of glory," ELW 705

## Looking back

Perhaps the greatest gift the disciples have given the church is not an example of perfect faith but their witness to human imperfection: how often they act not like wise saints, but ordinary, well-meaning people out of their depth—which, of course, they were.

It's hardly surprising that the disciples and the crowds struggled to grasp who Jesus really was, what his words and actions really meant. Jesus raised Lazarus from the dead, but he himself was humbled to the point of death on the cross. How could he be so easily defeated? It was unfathomable. Not until he rose again could people look back on what had happened and understand that through Jesus' death and resurrection, God broke the power of death for all people and for all time.

Looking back isn't always healthy, especially when nostalgia keeps us from recognizing God at work in the present. But it can help us to better understand the present and walk into the future. May God grant us wisdom and understanding, that our looking back will also lead us onward in a spirit of justice, compassion, and peace.

## Prayer

God of past, present, and future, we give you thanks that you are present with us in all times and places. By the power of your Spirit, may we face the past with honesty, the present with courage, and the future with hope. Amen.

## April 4

### John 12:23-25

[Jesus said,] "The hour has come for the Son of Man to be glorified. Very truly, I tell you, unless a grain of wheat falls into the earth and dies, it remains just a single grain; but if it dies, it bears much fruit. Those who love their life lose it, and those who hate their life in this world will keep it for eternal life."

### To ponder

One must not love oneself so much, as to avoid getting involved in the risks of life that history demands of us, and those that fend off danger will lose their lives, while those who out of love for Christ give themselves to the service of others will live.—Óscar Romero, homily, March 24, 1980

## Losing and living

These words of Jesus are not easy to understand. Clearly Jesus is alluding to what is about to happen to him: he will die, and through dying will "bear the fruit" of resurrection like a sea of grain. But what about loving our lives and therefore losing them, or hating our lives so that we keep them?

While we may never know for certain what Jesus meant, his reflection invites us to ponder not only what it means to die, but, more important, what it means to live. Perhaps it is as simple as this: when we are desperately clinging to life at all costs, wrapped up in a futile pursuit of avoiding age and death, that "life" we keep may be a grim and small one. To truly love life—to nurture and care for life as a beloved thing—is to be willing to "lose" it—to relinquish the need for control and to let our days flow into God's keeping. We may find that the more we "lose" our lives in wonder, in compassion, and in service, the more we find a life filled with grace—a life worth living.

## Prayer

God of life and death, give us courage to find what can only be discovered through letting go: trust in you, the joy of giving and service, and the grace that comes to us when we least expect it. Amen.

## April 5

### John 13:5, 12, 14

[Jesus] poured water into a basin and began to wash the disciples' feet and to wipe them with the towel that was tied around him. . . . After he had washed their feet, had put on his robe, and had returned to the table, he said to them, . . . "If I, your Lord and Teacher, have washed your feet, you also ought to wash one another's feet."

### To ponder

Believers who wash each other's feet show that they share in the body of Christ. They thus acknowledge their frequent need of cleansing, renew their willingness to let go of pride and worldly power, and offer their lives in humble service and sacrificial love.—Mennonite Church USA, "Confession of Faith"

## Love in action

Footwashing was not an unusual activity in first-century Palestine, where people often had to shed the dust of the roads they traveled before coming indoors. Jesus knelt to wash the feet of his disciples and instructed them to do the same, making this ordinary act something holy too.

In 2010 members of the Lutheran World Federation and Mennonite World Conference met together in Germany for an unprecedented action. The Lutheran assembly repented for Martin Luther's vitriolic writings against Anabaptist Christians, sentiments that long helped to fuel persecution against Anabaptist groups. In response, the Mennonite delegation presented the Lutherans with a handmade footwashing tub, signifying the central place of footwashing in the liturgy of many Anabaptist traditions. In a service of reconciliation, the leaders of both communities washed one another's feet.

Footwashing is a powerful symbol of the call for Christians to serve one another in humility and love. As Lutherans and Mennonites discovered after centuries of discord, it is never too late for confession, forgiveness, and reconciliation. It is never too late to wash one another's feet.

## Prayer

God of compassion, your overflowing love and grace washes over us. Give to your church a spirit of mutual care and service, in which we may receive and share your grace. Amen.

## April 6 / Maundy Thursday

### John 13:34-35

[Jesus said,] "I give you a new commandment, that you love one another. Just as I have loved you, you also should love one another. By this everyone will know that you are my disciples, if you have love for one another."

### To ponder

We are made for loving. If we don't love, we will be like plants without water.—Desmond Tutu, in "Celebrating Our Founders' 65th Anniversary"

## A new (old) commandment

It wasn't really a new commandment, of course. As many confirmation students could tell you, every one of the ten commandments is, at heart, an expression of love—love of God and love of our neighbors.

Moreover, the centrality of love in human relationships isn't unique to Christianity. World religions, philosophies, and popular culture alike reinforce the importance of love, and not only romantic love or a feeling of fondness, but love as an active commitment to the wellbeing of others.

Why, then, does Jesus call this commandment *new*? Perhaps because it's new to us. We haven't really tried it yet, except in fits and starts. After thousands of years of human conflict, loving one another is something we apparently still haven't managed to achieve.

Or maybe it's new because every time someone somewhere manages to love their neighbor as Jesus loves, the whole world is made new again, and the love we were made for is suddenly possible. Love, like water to a thirsty plant, can save our lives and renew the world.

## Prayer

Gracious God, the way of Jesus is the way of love, yet too often we choose a spirit of fear over your Spirit of love. Guide us and your world into the love that we were made for—the love of Jesus, which makes all things new. Amen.

## April 7 / Good Friday

John 19:16-18, 28-30

[The soldiers] took Jesus; and carrying the cross by himself, he went out to what is called The Place of the Skull, which in Hebrew is called Golgotha. There they crucified him. . . . [Jesus said,] "I am thirsty." A jar full of sour wine was standing there. So they put a sponge full of the wine on a branch of hyssop and held it to his mouth. When Jesus had received the wine, he said, "It is finished."

### To ponder

Faithful cross, true sign of triumph,
be for all the noblest tree;
none in foliage, none in blossom,
none in fruit your equal be;

symbol of the world's redemption,
for your burden makes us free.
—"Sing, my tongue," ELW 355

## Finished

Jesus was finished. No one could deny it. Despite such promise, such potential in his work, the cross had won. Grief overtook the disciples, who had given up everything to follow him, marginalized people who had dared to hope, and so many others who simply loved him and could not bear to imagine life without him. The world was suddenly as sour as the wine lifted to Jesus in his last moments before he said, "It is finished."

Jesus was finished. No one could deny it. The work he had come to do was not only about healing, teaching, signs, and miracles. From the moment of his incarnation as a newborn child, Jesus was God with us—in suffering, injustice, and tragedy, no less than in joy and triumph. In his death on the cross, Jesus walked with God's people to the very end—and beyond—so that in his resurrection, death itself was overturned by the power of God's love and grace. Already on Good Friday, the promise of Easter lived in Jesus' last words: It is finished!

## Prayer

God of the cross, whenever things look hopeless, you are there, already bringing life from death. Comfort all who mourn so that, even as we grieve, we remember your promise of resurrection. Amen.

## John 20:1, 16-18

Mary Magdalene came to the tomb and saw that the stone had been removed. . . . Jesus said to her, "Mary!" She turned and said to him in Hebrew, "Rabbouni!" (which means Teacher). Jesus said to her, "Do not hold on to me, because I have not yet ascended to the Father. But go to my brothers and say to them, 'I am ascending to my Father and your Father, to my God and your God.'" Mary Magdalene went and announced to the disciples, "I have seen the Lord."

## To ponder

The tomb being empty points to our now being full of the new life in Christ.—Jason Rocks, "The Significance of the Empty Tomb"

## It's empty!

Twelve preschoolers gathered impatiently around the island in the church kitchen. Following their Sunday School teacher's instructions, each child took a marshmallow and carefully wrapped it into crescent roll dough. "Just like Jesus was wrapped after he died," one girl solemnly repeated to herself, remembering the story. The finished products were placed in the heated oven and the door was firmly shut. Some minutes later the teacher removed the baked rolls from the oven. One by one, the preschoolers broke open their rolls and exclaimed, "It's empty!" The marshmallows had vanished, and only the sweetness remained.

Mary Magdalene expected death and found life; she expected grief and found joy. The resurrection of Jesus was an encounter between Jesus and those who loved him—a reunion that overturned all their logical expectations and replaced them with a new and childlike wonder.

In John's telling of this story, Mary Magdalene is first to meet and recognize the risen Christ, and first to be sent to share the good news of resurrection. Mary proclaimed, "I've seen the Lord!"—and those preschoolers echoed, in two words that could make a whole Easter sermon: "It's empty!"

## Prayer

God of resurrection, inspire in us the surprising joy of the empty tomb and the risen Christ. Fill our hearts with wonder, and with a love so abundant that it flows into every corner of our lives. Amen.

# Notes

**February 22:** T. S. Eliot, *Four Quartets* (Boston: Mariner, 1968). Henry Wadsworth Longfellow, 1807–1882, "A Psalm of Life." **February 23:** Text: John Newton, 1725–1807, alt., "Amazing grace, how sweet the sound," ELW 779, st. 1. **February 24:** Alice Meynell, "A General Communion," in *The Poems of Alice Meynell* (Toronto: McClelland and Stewart, 1923). Accessed on www.gutenberg.org/files/62251/62251-h/62251-h.htm. **February 25:** Traditional eucharistic prayer translated from the Latin "Agnus Dei." **February 26:** Martin Luther, "Luther's Small Catechism," *ELW*, 1164. **February 27:** Pope Francis, "Jesus' Invitation to 'Come and See,'" message by the Pope for the 55th World Communications Day, January 23, 2021, https://church.mt/jesus-invitation-to-come-and-see-message-by-the-pope-for-the-55th-world-communications-day/. **February 28:** William Shakespeare, *Romeo and Juliet*, Act II, Scene II. **March 1:** *Merriam Webster's Collegiate Dictionary*, 11th ed. (Springfield, MA: Merriam-Webster, 2005). **March 2:** "Holy Baptism," *ELW*, 230. **March 3:** Malcolm Guite, "Cleansing the Temple," *Sounding the Seasons* (Norwich: Canterbury, 2012). **March 4:** Text: Nikolai F. S. Grundtvig, 1783–1872, tr. Carl Doving, 1867–1937, adapt., "Built on a rock," ELW 652, st. 1. **March 5:** Abraham Joshua Heschel, *God in Search of Man* (New York: Harper & Row, 1955), 283. **March 6:** Rusty Edwards, "Let This Season Be," in *As Sunshine to a Garden* (Minneapolis: Augsburg Fortress, 1999), st. 1 and refrain. **March 7:** N. T. Wright, *Simply Christian* (New York: HarperCollins, 2006), 130. **March 8:** Martin Luther, *The Freedom of a Christian* (Minneapolis: Fortress, 2008), 67. **March 9:** Abraham Joshua Heschel, *God in Search of Man*, 124. **March 10:** Text: Thomas á Kempis, 1380–1471; tr. Benjamin Webb, 1819–1885, alt., "Oh, love, how deep," ELW 322, st. 1. **March 11:** James Cone, *The Cross and the Lynching Tree* (Maryknoll, NY: Orbis Books, 2011), Conclusion. **March 12:** "Sanitation Worker Angelo Bruno, 60, Talks with His Former Partner, Eddie Nieves, 55," in Dave Isay, *Callings: The Purpose and Passion of Work* (New York: Penguin, 2017), 127. **March 13:** Lee Hull Moses, *More than Enough* (Louisville: Westminster John Knox, 2016), 117. **March 14:** Dietrich Bonhoeffer, *Life Together* (New York: Harper Collins, 1954), 131. **March 15:** Michael Curry, *Love Is the Way* (New York: Avery, 2020), 61. **March 16:** Anne Lamott, *Hallelujah Anyway* (New York: Riverhead Books, 2017), 176. **March 17:** St. Basil the Great, in James Thornton, *Wealth and Poverty in the Teachings of the Church Fathers* (Berkeley, CA: St. John Chrysostom, 1993). **March 18:** Christine Sine, "Prayers for the Journey," in "Godspace" blog, September 21, 2013, https://godspace.wordpress.com/tag/prayers-for-the-journey/. **March 19:** Jean Vanier, in P. J. Clarke, *Lives that Made a Difference* (Durham, CT: Strategic, 2011), 198. **March 20:** Eugene Peterson, in Neil B. Wiseman, *The Pastor's Guide to Personal Spiritual Formation* (Boston: Beacon Hill Press, 2005), 134. Accessed at https://thepastorsworkshop.com/sermon-quotes-on-sabbath/. **March 21:** Maya Angelou, in *Rainbow in the Cloud* (New York: Random House, 2014), 68. **March 22:** John Berger, in "Ways of Seeing," essay 1, based on the 1972 BBC series. Accessed at www.ways-of-seeing.com/. **March 23:** Fyodor Dostoevsky, *The Brothers Karamazov*, trans. Constance Garnett (New York: Lowell Press, 2009), 708. **March 24:** Alicia Vargas, "Mujerismo and the Two Kin-Doms" *Dialog: A Journal of Theology*, vol. 49, no. 3, Fall 2010, 231–37. **March 25:** Branden Hunt, "Claimed by God through Baptism," *Living Lutheran*, June 26, 2018. Accessed at https://www.livinglutheran.org/2018/06/claimed-by-god-through-baptism/. **March 26:** Elie Wiesel, "Learning and Respect," commencement speech, June 15, 1997, DePaul University, Chicago. Accessed at https://bordeure.files.wordpress.com/2008/09/learning.pdf. **March 27:** Desmond Tutu, "10 Questions for Desmond Tutu," *TIME*, vol. 175, no. 11, March 22, 2010, p. 4. Accessed at http://content.time.com/time/subscriber/article /0,33009,1971410,00.html. **March 28:** Octavia Butler, *Parable of the Sower* (New York: Open Road Integrated Media, 2012). **March 29:** Sandra M. Schneiders, "Death in the Community of Eternal Life," *Interpretation: A Journal of Bible and Theology*, vol. 41 (1987), 54. **March 30:** Text: © 1996 Jeannette M. Lindholm, admin. Augsburg Fortress, "Before the waters nourished earth," ACS 1049, sts. 3 and 4. **March 31:** Eboni Marshall Turman, *Toward a Womanist Ethic of Incarnation* (London: Palgrave Macmillan, 2013), 172. **April 1:** Widely attributed to Martin Luther. **April 2:** Frederick Buechner, *A Room Called Remember* (New York: Harper & Row, 1984). **April 3:** Text: Harry E. Fosdick, 1878–1969, "God of grace and God of glory," ELW 705, st. 1. **April 4:** Óscar Romero, homily, March 24, 1980. **April 5:** Mennonite Church USA, "Confession of Faith in a Mennonite Perspective," Article 13: Foot Washing, www.mennoniteusa.org /who-are-mennonites/what-we-believe/confession-of-faith/foot-washing/. **April 6:** Desmond Tutu, in "Celebrating Our Founders' 65th Anniversary," Desmond and Leah Tutu Legacy Foundation, July 1, 2020, www.tutu.org.za/celebra ting-our-founders-65th-anniversary/. **April 7:** Text: Venantius Honorius Fortunatus, 530–609; tr. John Mason Neale, 1818–1866, alt., "Sing, my tongue," ELW 355, st. 6. **April 8:** Jason Rocks, "The Significance of the Empty Tomb," *Catholic Star Herald*, April 13, 2017, https://catholicstarherald.org/the-significance-of-the-empty-tomb/. For the activity mentioned, see "Empty Tomb Rolls," Around My Family Table blog, www.aroundmyfamilytable.com/empty-tomb-rolls-2/.